Original title: Embers of Time

Author: Sebastian Sarapuu
Editor: Jessica Elisabeth Luik
ISBN 978-9916-39-960-6

Embers of Time

Sebastian Sarapuu

Ashes of the Past

From the hearth where stories gleamed,
Rise the ashes of the past it seemed.
Memories in silent vast,
Hold the echoes of what's passed.

Beneath the soot, a glow persists,
Remnants of the joys and trysts.
Though time has flown fast,
We hold the ashes of the past.

Sunset Echoes

Crimson whispers in the sky
Golden hues where day does die
Clouds embrace with gentle hues
Shadows dance as light accrues

Mountains bask in fading glow
Nighttime's veil begins to grow
Stars emerge, their cold decree
Infinite in cosmic sea

Waves of light, a final hue
Dusk departs with rendezvous
Nature's quiet, evening's play
Sunset echoes day by day

Guiding Scars

Lines upon a weathered face
Map of life and endless chase
Memories etched in silent scars
Guiding light from distant stars

Paths we've tread and tears we've cried
Shaping hearts where love resides
Markers of our journeys passed
Strength and courage everlast

Struggles inked on fragile skin
Stories brave and worn within
Each line tells of battles fought
Lessons learned, wisdom brought

Bleeding Brilliance

Fractured light in twilight's grasp
Prism's break, yet hopes still clasp
Colors blend in bleeding sheen
Spectrum's dance, a vivid scene

Truth in shards of broken breath
Life anew in every death
Radiance in cracks revealed
Hidden strength, forever sealed

From the wounds, the brilliance bleeds
Nature's cycle, soul's own needs
In the fractures, beauty's mend
Light reborn at journey's end

Reflections in Ash

Whispers in the ashen air
Whirling ghosts of time declare
Life anew from ember's kiss
Phoenix rise, eternal bliss

Faded dreams in smoke entwined
Embers of a past defined
Scattered memories in the flame
Echoes rise, they speak my name

Flames consume but never end
In the ash, our souls amend
Reflections from the fire's edge
Rise as one with new-found pledge

Spiritual Glow

An aura lights the inner soul,
Reflecting grace in every whole.
Infinite peace, a gentle flow,
In twilight's hush, the spirit's glow.

Upon the dawn, where dreams compose,
A universe of quiet prose.
Eternal light begins to show,
In hearts that shine, the spirit's glow.

Last Luminescence

Fading light at evening's crest,
Whispers softly, granting rest.
The night, a canvas vast and dense,
Carries the last luminescence.

Sunset hues in golden trace,
Reflect the day in soft embrace.
As twilight shifts in gentle lens,
We hold the last luminescence.

Twinkling Remnants

In the night's embrace, stars ignite,
Tiny beacons, soft and bright.
Memories of days, remnants glow,
In twinkling light, they softly show.

Fleeting time in cosmic dance,
Every star a fleeting glance.
In vast expanse, we come to know,
Life's twinkling remnants, ebb and flow.

Endless Cinders

In the night where embers glare
Lost within the smoky air
Silent whispers, skies aflame
Ashes murmuring her name

Crimson sparks that never fade
Torching dreams where shadows played
Time's embrace on hollow wings
Burning tales that sorrow sings

Amongst the scattered fragments grey
Remnants of a sunlit day
Wisps of stories old and torn
From a life forever worn

Waning Light

Underneath a twilight veil
Stars ignite a frail detail
Glimmers where the darkness creeps
Waning light, a secret keeps

Moonlit echoes softly fall
Shadows dance in quiet thrall
Leaves whisper to the night
Hiding fears from fading sight

Midnight's breath with tender hand
Cradles dreams like grains of sand
As the dawn impatient waits
Hope in every heart creates

Gleaming Echoes

Through the valleys deep and wide
Gleaming echoes drift and glide
Memories of voices past
In the wind are gently cast

Mountains guard these ancient tales
Borne on wings of sweet travails
Songs that linger, echoes bright
In the heart, a steadfast light

Whispers from a time long gone
Hymns that greet the break of dawn
Through the ages, echoes gleam
Stitching life's enduring seam

Burnished Memories

Silver threads in autumn's air
Burnished memories' soft despair
Glimpses of a time most dear
Mirrored in a gentle tear

Amber leaves in silence speak
Whispers from a distant peak
Love's embrace in amber hue
Fading into skies of blue

Years like rivers swiftly flow
Secrets of a heart below
Gilded shadows, twilight's grace
Woven in our tender place

Amber Shadows

In the stillness of golden light,
Whispers of leaves in flight.
Amber shadows gently sway,
As the sun bids farewell to day.

Reflections of time bygone,
Captured in twilight's yawn.
Echoes of laughter and sorrow,
Promising dreams of tomorrow.

Silent whispers of ancient trees,
Humming melodies of the breeze.
Crickets serenade the night,
Basking in the amber light.

Twilit Remains

Lost in the hush of twilight,
Fading hues that softly bite.
Veil of dusk blankets the land,
As night extends its shadowed hand.

Stars ignite in the amber skies,
Whispers of day fade and die.
Crimson memories linger on,
Wrapped in the light of dawn.

Gentle echoes of the past,
In twilight, shadows cast.
Endings and beginnings find,
A place within the twilit mind.

Charred Histories

Ashes whisper tales unspoken,
Fragments of a world once broken.
Burned pages of time's story,
Echo realms of ancient glory.

Charred remains in silent rows,
Mark the paths that history knows.
Cinders dance in fleeting trace,
Of battles and forgotten grace.

From the flames arise anew,
Legends lost and shadows too.
In the embers' quiet glow,
Seeds of future stories grow.

Whispering Flames

Dancing flames in the midnight dark,
Flicker tales with a glowing spark.
Whispers in the crackling fire,
Hold secrets of heart's desire.

Blaze of colors fierce and bright,
Chasing shadows from the night.
Tongues of fire weave and twine,
Telling stories old as time.

In the embers' quiet fade,
Dreams and destinies are made.
Silent songs of light's embrace,
Echo in the fire's grace.

Glimpses Before Night

In the twilight's gentle embrace,
Shadows dance in soft caress.
Day bids farewell with tender grace,
As stars begin their evening press.

The sky, a canvas fading blue,
Whispers secrets of the dark.
With every hint of night's debut,
The moon ignites its silver spark.

Whispers of the evening breeze,
Carry tales of softened time.
Rustling through the swaying trees,
A silent, ancient pantomime.

Reflections on the river's crest,
Diamond fragments in the flow.
Lull the world to peaceful rest,
In the twilight's lovely glow.

Cinders of Moments

Flickers of the past ignite,
In the hearth of memory.
Ashes of a distant light,
Still hold warmth and poetry.

Embers trace the stories old,
In the quiet of the night.
Tales in shadows softly told,
Glowing remnants burning bright.

Sparks of laughter once alive,
Fade in cinders' gentle hue.
Yet in hearts they still revive,
Breathing life to moments true.

Time, a flame that dims and flares,
Caught in whispers of the fire.
Through the darkened space it dares,
Leaving trails of soft desire.

Slowly Dimming

Golden hues give way to gray,
As the sun retreats to sleep.
Dusk extends its quiet sway,
Spreading shadows, soft and deep.

Colors blend and softly fade,
Into twilight's tender shroud.
Lost in evening's calm parade,
Stars unveil their sparkling crowd.

Every whisper, every sigh,
Echoes through the cooling night.
Silent as the shadows fly,
Following the waning light.

Dreams arise with newfound grace,
In the arms of dimming eve.
As if time begins to pace,
Hands that gently weave and leave.

Last Light

Beneath the canopy of stars,
Where the shadows softly lie.
Whispers linger from afar,
Painting stories in the sky.

Final rays of sunshine gleam,
Kissing earth with fleeting glow.
Fading like a distant dream,
Into twilight's tender flow.

Every moment gently sways,
Caught in evening's tranquil breath.
Brushing past the waning days,
As dusk settles into depth.

Candles flicker in the dusk,
Echoes of the fiery sun.
In the night, we gently trust,
That a new day soon will come.

Cindered Chronicles

In ashen tales where shadows speak,
An ember's glow reveals the meek,
From ruins rise a phoenix call,
In cindered dreams, we stand tall.

Through soot and smoke, the past unwinds,
Forgotten lore in tattered binds,
Each spark ignites the haunted maze,
As cindered night births brighter days.

Ghostly whispers in the twilight,
Ancient paths that seek the light,
Embers dance on winds unswayed,
In cindered hearts, courage laid.

Luminescent Whispers

In twilight's grasp, soft secrets weave,
Luminescent whispers deceive,
Moonlight's kiss on silken streams,
Guardians of our tranquil dreams.

Glowing shades in twilight's dress,
Silent murmurs, night caress,
Echoes of a starlit time,
Luminescence in whispers prime.

Shadows melt in dawn's embrace,
Whispers fade without a trace,
Yet the glow of night remains,
In luminescent whispers, refrains.

Scintillating Eons

Through the veil of endless years,
Scintillating eons persevere,
Eternal dance of cosmic flow,
In the stars, our stories grow.

Galaxies in grand parade,
Nebulae in colors displayed,
Time's tapestry, a boundless scroll,
Scintillations heal the soul.

Universes intertwine,
Infinite and so divine,
In eon's glow, we find our place,
Scintillating in boundless space.

Glimmering Fragments

From shattered past, fragments glow,
Glimmering tales in twilight's flow,
Every piece a story told,
In fragments, glimmers of old.

Lights that flicker, soft and frail,
Whispers of a distant trail,
Glimmering in the moon's serene,
Fragments of what we have seen.

Each broken shard, a memory,
In glimmering light, set free,
Piecing together a luminous fate,
In fragments, glimmers await.

Vestiges of Yesterday

In the shadows of time long passed,
Whispered secrets softly cast,
Echoes linger of days once bright,
Fading gently into night.

Through the corridors of faded grace,
Memories hide, a silent embrace,
Etched in stone, stories lay,
Vestiges of a distant day.

A tapestry of moments gone,
Woven through the light of dawn,
Threads of gold and silver grey,
Tales of yesterdays replay.

Paths once walked in twilight's hue,
Beneath skies of endless blue,
Now just shadows, softly sway,
In the remnants of the day.

Smoldering Days

In the ember's gentle glow,
Stories of the past bestow,
Whispers of a time once knew,
In these flames, the old renew.

Flickers dance in silent night,
Casting dreams in soft moonlight,
Smoldering days leave their mark,
In the ash, a fading spark.

Through the quiet of the dusk,
Memories rise, a gentle musk,
Breath of yore in smoky haze,
Lingering in twilight phase.

Burning slow, the moments pass,
In the mirror of the glass,
Reflecting times of love and grace,
In these smoldering days, a trace.

Faint Glows

Under the stars, a soft embrace,
Faint glows leave a gentle trace,
In the night, whispers confide,
Tales of love, horizons wide.

Twilight's kiss on twilight's brow,
Moments linger, here and now,
In the silence, secrets bloom,
Light the shadows, pierce the gloom.

Softly glistens morning dew,
Reflecting days both old and new,
Glimmers of what once has been,
Shining bright, though faint and thin.

In the heart's secluded place,
Memories time cannot erase,
Flickers in a soft repose,
In the quiet, faint glows.

Nostalgic Sparks

In the fireplace, they ignite,
Memories of nights so bright,
Nostalgic sparks in fleeting dance,
In their glow, we find a chance.

Whispers of the fire's grace,
Echoes in the silent space,
Radiant beams of yesteryear,
Flicker softly, reappear.

Hearts remember, souls entwine,
Stories of a distant time,
Sparks that lit the darkest night,
Now a gentle, softened light.

In the ember's warm embrace,
Dreams of lore find their place,
Nostalgic sparks, vivid brief,
In their glow, there lies relief.

Ephemeral Radiance

Moments shimmer then fade
like stars at the brink of dawn
Illusions dance in the night
by morning, they're withdrawn

A promise of golden light
paints skies of azure hue
But time's relentless march
dims the brightest view

Whispers cling to twilight
echoes of past night's song
Fragile threads of memory
in the wind, they belong

Love's fleeting embrace
as shadows kiss daylight's end
Ephemeral radiance fades
and dreams descend

In the heart's deep recess
silent wishes reside
Evanescent beams of hope
forever our guide

Nostalgic Glow

In the amber light of eve
memories softly tread
Whispers of days gone by
dance in the heart's stead

Old photographs yellowing
imprint the past's embrace
Shadows of cherished moments
on the soul's silent face

Childhood's laughter echoes
through halls of distant days
Tangible as morning mist
yet like smoke, it strays

Faded letters from yore
with inked love remain
A testament to yesteryears
and whispers of refrain

Under the crescent moon
nostalgic glow so pure
In the quiet of the night
our hearts find their cure

Seared Remnants

Burned bridges stand silent
against a crimson sky
Ashes of dreams and hopes
in the wind, they lie

Scorched earth beneath our feet
remains of love's past flame
Echoes of what once was
there's no one to blame

Shattered pieces of trust
like glass, lay strewn around
Silent witnesses to pain
on this battleground

Bitter memories linger
within the charred remains
Yet from this desolation
a new strength is gained

Out of sorrow's dark night
resilience takes root
From seared remnants of love
a rebirth does shoot

Fleeting Fires

In the gleam of twilight
passions brightly ignite
Fleeting fires of desire
burn intensely, then take flight

Moments of fervent blaze
reflections in your eyes
Embers hot and fierce
till the morning rise

Words of love whispered
in the hush of night
Promises of forever
but gone with dawn's light

Brief encounters of flame
leave a mark on the soul
Ephemeral yet profound
they make us whole

As the fires subside
the sparks still remain
In the heart's quiet nook
awaiting the next flame

Desolate Illumination

In barren lands, the shadows creep,
Where sun has set, the night is deep.
Yet one lone star dares still to gleam,
A dim reminder of a dream.

The moonlight kisses empty grounds,
The silence here, it has no bounds.
But in the stillness, whispers wane,
Of light once loved and hopes in vain.

Ghostly beams, they forge a trail,
Through desolation, pale and frail.
A lantern guiding souls astray,
In search of dawn and clearer day.

The echoes of forgotten light,
Glimmer faintly in the night.
A beacon in the void of space,
That keeps alive a fleeting trace.

Fleeting Brilliance

A comet blazes through the sky,
It's gone in just the blink of eye.
A moment's spark, a flash so dear,
Lost to time, yet shining clear.

A butterfly flits, colors bright,
Its wings a canvas, pure delight.
Yet brief its dance, a transient show,
In precious hues that swiftly go.

Cherry blossoms bloom, then fall,
Their petals soft, ephemeral.
In springtime's breath, they burst and cheer,
But soon they fade, their end is near.

A rainbow arcs through mist and rain,
A spectrum bright, then gone again.
Its fleeting brilliance, short and sweet,
A promise grand, a rare treat.

Belated Resplendence

From dawn delayed, the sun ascends,
A glow renewed, as night's veil ends.
The sky ablaze with morning's light,
Belated daybreak, pure and bright.

In time's embrace, the flowers bloom,
Late but lush, dispelling gloom.
Their colors rich, a sight to see,
Belated gift of majesty.

A star ignites in twilight hours,
Its glow delayed, yet still it showers.
Celestial fire in night's embrace,
A tardy spark of endless grace.

Though late, the splendor does arrive,
A vivid force that keeps alive.
In resplendence, beauty stays,
Despite the hours or the days.

Citrine Murmurs

Whispers drift through golden glade,
Where citrine streams in sunlight fade.
Leafy canopies, they sway,
In murmurs sweet, the breezes play.

Amber-hued, the forest sings,
With gentle notes that twilight brings.
Each ray of light, a tender kiss,
In citrine's touch, a perfect bliss.

Warmth of day, so softly glows,
Through branches green, where silence flows.
The whispers weave a tapestry,
Of nature's love and harmony.

In citrine hues, the world is hushed,
With murmurs soft, the leaves are brushed.
A symphony in golden light,
That serenades the coming night.

Radiant Echoes

In the quiet dawn, light softly sings,
Whispers of time in golden beams.
Memories dance on gossamer wings,
In a world sewn from wistful dreams.

Echoes ripple through fields and seas,
Gleaming bright where shadows lay.
Nature's chorus, a gentle breeze,
Carries the past to the break of day.

Laughter lingers in silent spaces,
Born anew on morning's glow.
Hearts recall those cherished faces,
In the echoes of long ago.

Beneath the azure, a symphony,
Of life and love, entwined, aglow.
Radiant echoes of eternity,
Through time and tide, forever flow.

Aglow with Hindsight

Hindsight's flame, a lantern bright,
Illuminates the winding path.
Through the mist of memory's night,
We find the strength to face the wrath.

Choices made on life's great stage,
Engraved in heart and thought.
In reflection, we turn the page,
Lessons learned, and battles fought.

Aglow, the past like jewels gleam,
In the tapestry of years.
Weaving through each dream and scheme,
Binding joy and silent tears.

Guided by the light we've known,
We tread with wiser, steadier stride.
For in the glow, the seeds are sown,
Of futures bright, where hopes reside.

Crimson Reflections

Sunset paints the sky in scarlet hues,
A canvas vast, where dreams take flight.
Crimson reflections in endless views,
Within the dance of fading light.

Beneath the twilight, shadows stretch,
To touch the night with tender grace.
In the heart, the memories etch,
A story told in time's embrace.

Leaves of amber whisper low,
As evening folds the day to rest.
The stars emerge in gentle flow,
Crimson echoes in the west.

Reflections of the days gone by,
Sculpted in the evening's fire.
In the silence, our spirits fly,
Toward the dawn of new desire.

Cinders of Yesterday

Amid the ashes, whispers rise,
Of days now gone, of lives once full.
Cinders of yesterday, beneath the skies,
Hold stories in their dusky pull.

The flames once bright, now softly fade,
But warmth remains in hearts aglow.
In embers' light, the paths we made,
Guide us through the night's tableau.

Each ember tells of love and loss,
Of dreams ablaze and shadows cast.
In cinders, we find what we emboss,
The echoes of a wistful past.

From the ashes, new sparks take flight,
Renewed by time and endless grace.
Cinders of yesterday's gentle light,
Illumine every soul's embrace.

Lingering Flare

In the twilight's gentle grasp,
Shadows dance in soft embrace.
Lighting skies with one last gasp,
Sparks dissolve without a trace.

Rays of gold in fading light,
Brush the world with tender care.
As the day turns into night,
In the dusk, a lingering flare.

Memories in amber hue,
Whisper tales of bygone days.
Echoed dreams of skies once blue,
Now just shadows in the haze.

Fleeting moments drift away,
Caught between the now and then.
Silent whispers, night and day,
Fade like echoes in the glen.

Aged Radiance

On the edge of time's old shore,
Ocean waves of gold do gleam.
Whisper truths of evermore,
In the twilight's gentle dream.

Wrinkles trace a path of life,
Etched with moments, joy, and pain.
Years of laughter, days of strife,
In the old sun's last refrain.

Golden hues upon the face,
Lines of wisdom, tales untold.
In each crease, a soft embrace,
Wonders of a life of gold.

Through the lens of seasoned eyes,
Stars align in fading glow.
Radiance aged, never dies,
In the heart, time moves slow.

Dwindling Glow

In the depth of night's embrace,
Faintest beams begin to wane.
Softly fading, losing trace,
Of the sun's enduring reign.

Candle's light in shadows cast,
Whispers of a stolen past.
Illuminates what once was vast,
Till twilight's grip is strong and fast.

Every spark that once was bright,
Now succumbs to velvet dark.
Falling stars in silent flight,
Leave but dust and ancient mark.

Moments linger, soft and slow,
In this gentle ebb and flow.
As the daylight starts to go,
Nurtured by a dwindling glow.

Final Ember

In the hearth's dying embrace,
Embers whisper low and soft.
Memories in glowing grace,
Float like dreams to skies aloft.

Fading warmth in twilight's breath,
Crackling echoes fill the air.
Moments linger, life and death,
In the dusk, their final flare.

Shadows play upon the wall,
Dancing through the night so still.
In their trace, a silent call,
From the ember's dying thrill.

As the last spark fades from sight,
Into night, the world descends.
In the quietude of night,
Every ending, time defends.

Smoldering Memories

In twilight's whisper, echoes stay,
A dance of shadows, soft and gray.
The past is warm, yet distant too,
A spark that fades from whence it grew.

Old laughter haunts the silent night,
In dreams, it flickers, faint and bright.
Sweet voices call from yesteryears,
Their tender whispers, silent tears.

Each ember glows with stories told,
Of joys and sorrows, tales of old.
A touch, a glance, the way things were,
In silence now, they softly stir.

These memories, though dim, they stay,
In heart and soul, they find their way.
Though time may blur and distance grow,
Forever in our hearts, they glow.

Fading Glows

In twilight's ebb, the daylight wanes,
The sun retreats, yet warmth remains.
The evening brings a gentle peace,
As shadows grow and whispers cease.

The ember's glow, it softly dies,
A fleeting light 'neath velvet skies.
Each fading flame a silent sigh,
A whispered wish, a last goodbye.

The world spins on, yet moments cling,
To fading echoes, memories sing.
Within the darkness, light has gone,
Yet in our hearts, it lingers on.

Time gently fades, and so do we,
A dance with shadows, endlessly.
Yet in this twilight, love still shows,
Amidst the quiet, fading glows.

Lingering Flames

In the hearth, a fire holds,
Whispering secrets, stories old.
The flames, they dance, a vibrant glow,
In quiet rooms, their warmth does show.

Each spark a dream, a hope, a sigh,
A fleeting wish 'neath starlit sky.
In tender light, the shadows play,
As night consumes the fading day.

The fire speaks in crackling tones,
Of ancient lands and distant homes.
In each bright flare, a memory lies,
A fragment of the past that flies.

Though flames may wane, their essence stays,
In ghostly light of yesterdays.
In heart and mind, their echo frames,
The soft, enduring, lingering flames.

Eternal Cinders

In the ashes lies a tale,
Of dreams pursued, of quests that fail.
Eternal cinders softly gleam,
In twilight's glow, a whispered dream.

From the fire's end, new light is born,
In silent night, in break of morn.
Each ember bright, a distant star,
A beacon near, a guide afar.

Though flames may die, their spirit stays,
In heart and thought, through endless days.
In every cinder, life anew,
A spark of hope, a flame in view.

In ashes cold, we find our way,
Through darkest night to break of day.
Eternal cinders, timeless art,
An endless fire within the heart.

Glowing Elements

In the silence of the night,
Stars whisper secrets old and bright,
Elements dance in cosmic flame,
Nature's tune, forever the same.

Through the air, a flicker of light,
Guiding dreams in silent flight,
The earth beneath, a steady guide,
In whom all forms of life confide.

Water's kiss on stones so pure,
Nurturing life with a touch so sure,
A fiery core, hidden deep,
Where all the ancient secrets sleep.

Ay, the wind, a wandering muse,
Singing tales of ancient views,
Each element, a symphony,
In nature's grandest harmony.

Radiant Continuum

Eternal light, through eons shine,
A radiant continuum, divine,
Across the ages, unbroken stream,
Weaving the fabric of every dream.

Through the veil of time we go,
Like rivers in an endless flow,
Moments caught in a golden thread,
Binding all the lives we've led.

Day and night, a seamless dance,
Filled with wonder, filled with chance,
In every sphere, a luminous trace,
Of the infinite time and space.

Each dawn's kiss, a promise told,
Within the heart of the bold,
To see beyond the fleeting day,
And chase the eternal's glowing ray.

Gleaming Reflections

Mirrors of life, in silent gleam,
Reflecting dreams, like a midnight stream,
The moon above, a watchful eye,
Witness to the ebb and sigh.

In a glance, a story lies,
Of hidden truths and whispered cries,
Every tear, a crystal bright,
Carrying fragments of the night.

Surface calm, but depths untold,
Where mysteries begin to unfold,
Reflections speak, in silent tone,
Of worlds beyond our own.

Through the light, see what's concealed,
Inner secrets slowly revealed,
Gleaming paths, in moonlit hues,
Guiding us with ancient clues.

Ashen Hours

In shadows cast by twilight's veil,
Ashen hours begin their tale,
Silent whispers fill the air,
Of life's moments, tender and rare.

Time stands still in muted gray,
As dreams of night hold gentle sway,
Each second marked by quiet grace,
In this calm, unhurried space.

From embers bright, to darkened glow,
Life's cycles turn, ebb, and flow,
Within the hour, truth lays bare,
In its ashen, tranquil stare.

The silent hush, an endless charm,
Offering solace, keeping warm,
In the hours soft with dust,
We find a peace, we learn to trust.

Burning Shadows

In twilight's tender grip, we dance
To shadows' burning, fierce romance
Flames flicker in the dusk's embrace
Night's curtain falls, a solemn grace

Whispers ride on summer's breeze
Carrying secrets through the trees
Illuminated paths we tread
As shadows' flames paint skies in red

Ghosts of daylight drift away
Leaving dark, where bright lights play
Moonlight smiles on quiet streets
Where silence and the twilight meet

Stars ignite the inky skies
Burning shadows, whispered lies
Reflections of what once was light
Echo softly through the night

The nightingale's song softly trills
Through valleys, over silent hills
In fires burning, shadows signed
A dance of dream, of unseen binds

Silent Ashes

Silent ashes whisper tales
Of dreams that sailed on bygone gales
Embers cold and grey remain
Of fires that once no chains could tame

In moments lost, in time's deep hold
The stories of the past unfold
Light, now dim, still softly glows
In silent ashes' quiet prose

Beneath the moon's unyielding stare
Soft ashes lie, stripped, bare
Silent songs of what has passed
In shadows' depths, the echoes cast

Memories like ghostly shrouds
Beneath the weight of time's grey clouds
In silent ashes, whispers tire
Of passions' past and lost desires

From ashes to the whispering air
Ephemeral dreams take gentle care
To drift where silent echoes roam
And find in future, seeds of home

Forgotten Glimmers

In the corners of our minds they gleam
Forgotten glimmers of a dream
Memories faded, softly glow
In shadows where we dare not go

Old stars that once had brightly shone
Now linger, memories nearly gone
In heart's recess, they sleep, confined
Till whispers wake them from the mind

Time's river flows, erodes the shore
Yet glimmers shine, forevermore
In sepia tones, they softly fade
Reminders of the joys we made

Echoes of laughter, whispers, tears
Glimmers traced by lost, young years
They flicker in the mind's deep well
Soft stories now, once tales to tell

Dreams of times long past, still clear
They softly whisper in our ear
With each forgotten glimmer's light
We find the stars that fill our night

Timeless Sparks

In moments fleeting, sparks ignite
They light the path through endless night
Timeless in their fleeting flair
In shadows cast, they light the air

A spark is born in heart's deep core
A light to carry, to explore
Through ages past and futures bright
These sparks defy the darkest night

Eyes that sparkle, hearts that flare
Timeless sparks are everywhere
In laughter's sound, in love's embrace
In fleeting moments we retrace

They guide us through the passage vast
Connecting future, present, past
In every joy and every fear
Timeless sparks will reappear

Eternal glow in every spark
A guide to light us through the dark
In timeless sparks, we find our way
Through every night to break of day

Lucid Recollections

In the silent depths of night,
Memories weave tapestries bright.
Ghosts of moments softly call,
Echoes of what we once saw.

Under moon's pale, watchful eye,
Dreams return, no need to try.
Whispers from the past arise,
As stardust fills the midnight skies.

Eyes closed, the visions clear,
Time collapses, drawing near.
Hands reach out to shadows past,
Blurry edges fading fast.

Softly, gently, thoughts unfold,
Stories in our hearts retold.
In the deep and silent night,
Lucid dreams take wondrous flight.

Ember-lit Pathways

Through the forest dim and old,
Tales of lore and myths are told.
Embers light the shadowed way,
Guiding us to break of day.

Ancient trees, a watchful guard,
Secrets whispered, ever hard.
Footsteps trace where legends walked,
Under boughs where dragons talked.

Softly hum the winds of time,
Nature's song, profound and prime.
Through the darkness, gems ignite,
Paths of fire in the night.

Lost and found in wood so deep,
Where the quiet shadows creep.
Ember trails to guide us home,
Through the places dreams do roam.

Stellar Residues

In the vast expanse above,
Stars leave traces, whispers of love.
Fragments of celestial dreams,
Floating in the cosmic streams.

Galaxies swirl in silent song,
To the universe we belong.
Ancient light from distant shores,
Legacy of far-off wars.

Particles of bygone stars,
Dance in space, traverse the scars.
Universe in grand design,
Mapped in stardust, line by line.

Eternal echoes, cosmic breath,
Life and death in twinkling heft.
In the night's vast solitude,
We are all but stellar residues.

Frozen Infernos

In the heart of icy realms,
Fire and ice take up the helms.
Blazing frost and cold that burns,
Nature's paradox, it churns.

Snowflakes dance in embered breeze,
Heat and chill in perfect ease.
Molten rivers under ice,
Duality's intricate device.

Life persists in frozen fire,
Thriving in the hot desire.
Elemental wars within,
Peace where opposites begin.

Mystic lands where contrasts meet,
Where the cold and fervor greet.
Frozen infernos, wild and free,
Nature's ultimate decree.

Fading Firelight

In the dimming glow of night,
Softly hums a song of light,
Whispers dance with shadows' might,
Fading fire, a fleeting sight.

Crackling embers, whispers low,
Tales of days both fast and slow,
Memories in the twilight flow,
Gentle as the evening's glow.

Cloaked in warmth, the heart takes flight,
Beneath the stars that share their light,
Dreams awaken, pure and bright,
In the fading firelight.

Silent breezes weave and shiver,
By the hearth where moments quiver,
Time's relentless, ceaseless river,
Carries flames that once did glitter.

Night enfolds the fading spark,
Fires dim, but leave their mark,
In the quiet, in the dark,
Lingers still the fire's arc.

Whispers in the Ashes

From the shadows deep and gray,
Ancient voices gently sway,
Whispers in the ashes play,
Secrets of a bygone day.

Ghostly murmurs, soft and low,
Chronicles from long ago,
In the silence, stories flow,
Ashes tell what once did glow.

Lingering where paths diverge,
Underneath the twilight's urge,
Voices from the past emerge,
In the ashes' quiet surge.

Wisdom in the dust confined,
Fragments of a grand design,
In the ashes we can find,
Echoes of another time.

Remembered through the softest sighs,
As the moon begins to rise,
Whispers in the ashes lie,
Silent under midnight skies.

Echoes at Dusk

When the sun begins to wane,
And the shadows stretch again,
Echoes whisper soft, inane,
At the edge of twilight's reign.

Hazy hues of purple skies,
Mirror tales of lost goodbyes,
Memories that never die,
Speak in echoes, soft replies.

Silent moments, gentle breach,
Wars and wonders, out of reach,
In the echoes, they beseech,
Dusk imparts what dreams beseech.

In the twilight's tender hue,
All the world feels fresh and new,
Echoes whisper what is true,
In the dusk, for me and you.

Time recedes, the night's incline,
Stars and moon in grand design,
Echoes at dusk intertwine,
With the heart and soul's align.

Flickers of Memory

Faintest sparks within our mind,
Tiny flames from days behind,
Flickers of memory we find,
Stories in the heart confined.

Moments dance in golden light,
Shadowed edges, whispers bright,
In the quiet of the night,
Memories take their flight.

Through the ages, soft they burn,
Lessons lived and love discern,
In their glow, we twist and turn,
To the past, our hearts return.

From the dark, the light will glean,
Visions of what might have been,
Flickers of a distant dream,
Flowing in a seamless stream.

Every ember, every spark,
Guides us through the fading dark,
In the flickers we embark,
Tracing back to where we start.

Flickers of Yesterday

In the whispers of twilight's sighs,
We glimpse the echoes of our youth.
A tale of time that's drifting by,
Masking the unspoken truth.

Through the veil of misty dawn,
Memories shimmer, then they fade.
Moments lost and then reborn,
In the skies that evening made.

Gentle whispers in the air,
Carry traces of the past.
How we yearn to linger there,
In a dream that cannot last.

Footprints on forgotten shores,
Silent songs the heart can play.
In the quiet, love restores,
Flickers of our yesterday.

Incandescent Dreams

In the realm of slumber's light,
Where the stars within us gleam,
We embark on flights of night,
Into worlds of purest dream.

Candles of the mind ignite,
Casting shadows soft and bright.
Every wish takes wondrous flight,
In the silence of the night.

Mirrors of our deepest fears,
Set alight with hopeful beams.
They dissolve like morning's tears,
Leaving only incandescent dreams.

Skies of gold, and seas of glass,
Whispers of the cosmic streams.
In this land where moments pass,
We live on in glowing dreams.

Candescent Histories

In the scrolls of time we find,
Stories etched in fire and light.
Every epoch's heart entwined,
With both day and deepest night.

Embodied in the tales we weave,
Echoes of our joy and pain.
Chronicles the years conceive,
In the sunshine and the rain.

Histories like beacons shine,
Guiding through the stormy seas.
In their warmth, our souls align,
With their ancient melodies.

Each tale a candle in the dark,
Illuminating paths unseen.
In their glow, we leave our mark,
On the canvas of the dream.

Warm Ruins

Among the ruins of our past,
Lie the embers, glowing still.
Even stones worn down and vast,
Whisper tales of iron will.

Walls that stood the test of time,
Now a testament to grace.
In their shadow, hearts do climb,
Finding love in every trace.

Even in the wreckage warm,
Life and hope begin anew.
Petals bloom against the storm,
Colors burst where shadows grew.

Amidst the rubble, dreams are spun,
Kindled by the ember's gleam.
Warm the ruins 'neath the sun,
Harboring a timeless dream.

Echoes in Coal

In the depths of darkness, stories unfold,
Where whispers of time in shadows are sold.
Miners of memory, diggers of yore,
Unearth the past in coal's silent roar.

Echoes resound in blackened veins,
Lives intertwined in soot and stains.
Forgotten songs of toil and strife,
Breathing through the cracks of night.

Buried voices, they wail and plea,
A chorus of ghosts in a ceaseless sea.
Hammers strike to forgotten beat,
In the catacombs where past and present meet.

Coal's embrace is cold yet warm,
Cradling tales of endless storm.
In the heart of earth, histories merge,
Silent witnesses to nature's dirge.

Glimmers of light in the black abyss,
Fragments of hope, sweet as a kiss.
Echoes in coal, eternal refrain,
Binding moments of joy and pain.

Vestigial Flames

Once proud fires that danced so high,
Now flicker faintly against the sky.
Ghosts of embers, embered hues,
Quietly whispering ancient truths.

Heat of passion, once so bright,
Now a memory in the night.
Dreams of yonder, time has claimed,
Left but vestiges, fires untamed.

Smoldering fragments, ashes creep,
Through the silence, secrets seep.
Tales of old in shadows play,
Vestigial flames in twilight's sway.

Murmur of flames, soft embrace,
Time-worn faces, tender grace.
Ephemeral spark of bygone days,
Fading softly in twilight's rays.

Yet in each spark, a promise gleams,
Hope rekindled in quiet dreams.
Vestigial flames, a silent vow,
Lighting paths to the here and now.

Twilight's Glow

The skies bleed hues of lavender and gold,
A canvas painted, stories unfold.
Daylight fades to night's embrace,
In twilight's glow, time leaves no trace.

Shadows lengthen, secrets bloom,
Stars emerge from the silent gloom.
The world whispers, soft and low,
In the tender hum of twilight's glow.

Moments suspended in the dusky air,
Dreams take flight, free from care.
Boundaries blur, heartbeats slow,
In the ethereal light of twilight's glow.

Memories dance, ephemeral and true,
Wrapped in the twilight's shifting hue.
Breath of night in a gentle flow,
Circling back in twilight's glow.

Hope and sorrow, hand in hand,
Tread softly on twilight's land.
A promise kept, a seed to sow,
Eternity whispers in twilight's glow.

Glimmering Ruins

Among the rubble, stories hide,
Whispers of ages in each stride.
Broken walls, crumbling stones,
Echoing with forgotten tones.

In the dust of time, treasures lie,
Shards of dreams beneath the sky.
Silent sentinels, shadows cast,
Glimmering ruins of the past.

Rays of sun through windows bare,
Cast a glow on the memories there.
Amidst decay, beauty blooms,
Life breathes in forgotten rooms.

Each ruin tells a tale anew,
Of lives once lived, of skies once blue.
Glimmer of hope, in the decay,
History's touch in night's soft sway.

From the ruins, wisdom grows,
A legacy in the wind that blows.
Glimmering ruins, hearts that soar,
Whispering secrets forevermore.

Rekindled Moments

Under twilight's gentle hue,
Memories like whispers, old and new,
Hearts once closed, now open wide,
Past dreams drift back with the tide.

Glimmers of laughter, echoes so clear,
Kisses soft, once held dear,
In these moments, love is found,
Souls rekindled, no longer bound.

Glances stolen in moon's embrace,
Time and space, we now retrace,
Holding close what time has healed,
In rekindled moments, truth is revealed.

Whispers of the autumn breeze,
Secrets shared in rustling trees,
In the spark of twilight's dance,
Two hearts beat in sweet expanse.

Through the window of the soul's gaze,
We find light in darkened days,
Each spark a testament to,
Rekindled moments between me and you.

Scorched Hours

The sun's relentless, burning rays,
Count the hours, tuck away,
Shadows dance on parched lands,
Time slips through blistered hands.

Sweat and toil under skies so blue,
Dreams evaporate in heat's cruel view,
No refuge found, no sweet relief,
Only scorched hours and silent grief.

Each second stretches, an endless plight,
Day turns to dusk without respite,
The earth sighs, cracked and dry,
Under scorched hours, beneath the sky.

In the night, the coolness creeps,
O'er slumbered days and restless sleeps,
Awakening whispers of the breeze,
Easing scars, putting minds at ease.

Yet when dawn breaks, the fire resumes,
A burning clock till the day consumes,
In scorched hours we find our test,
Seeking solace, seeking rest.

Illuminated Past

In golden glow of bygone days,
Light pours in with warming rays,
Each memory etched in pristine light,
Illuminated past, so vivid, bright.

Through the haze of time, we see,
Moments etched in clarity,
Faces, places, love so deep,
In illuminated past, memories keep.

Faint laughter carried on the breeze,
Whispers of youthful, carefree ease,
In the glow of twilight's cast,
We cherish the illuminated past.

Warm embraces, tender sighs,
Reflected in the midnight skies,
Stars align, our hearts hold fast,
To the beauty of the illuminated past.

In each gleam, a tale retold,
Of days gone by, in hearts ensouled,
Through times veil, we peer and bask,
In the light of the illuminated past.

Vanishing Gleams

In the quiet hush of night's embrace,
Gleams of light begin to trace,
Softly fading into streams,
Vanishing into fleeting dreams.

Whispers of stars, distant and shy,
Glimmering in the darkened sky,
One by one, they disappear,
Vanishing gleams, crystal clear.

Ephemeral sparks, moments fleeting,
In their light, hearts are meeting,
But shadows inch with silent schemes,
Stealing away those vanishing gleams.

The moonlight wanes, a silver tear,
Reflecting hopes and dormant fears,
In the dance of night's regimes,
Chasing the echoes of vanishing gleams.

Till dawn breaks with blushing hue,
A canvas bright, a world anew,
Yet in our dreams, we'll always see,
The vanishing gleams of memories.

Charred Epochs

History's scrolls, in embered stacks,
Dreams of yore, now shadow's tracks,
Ashes whisper tales untold,
In the silence, secrets unfold.

Empires rose, and empires fell,
Stone by stone, the bygone world,
Upon the winds, the silent knell,
Charred epochs, in darkness curled.

Ages burned by time's cruel hand,
Wisdom lost in shifting sand,
In every spark, a story writ,
In every cinder, shadows flit.

Ghosts of glory in the dust,
Memories in every gust,
Stoking flames of past undone,
Yet tonight, their echoes run.

Thus we stand on ashen ground,
Listening for the smallest sound,
Through charred epochs, we survey,
Echoes of the yesterday.

Dwindling Light

Twilight weaves its subtle spell,
Night awaits with tales to tell,
Dwindling light, the day's last sigh,
Beneath a dark, unfolding sky.

Shadows dance upon the breeze,
Moon ascends between the trees,
Stars emerge in quiet flight,
Painting dreams, soft and bright.

Fading hues on heaven's dome,
Guiding us towards night's home,
In the dim, the beauty's found,
Silent whispers all around.

Lanterns glow in twilight's hand,
Guiding footsteps on the land,
In the dusk, we find our way,
In the dusk, we're led astray.

Embrace the night, the calm it brings,
Listen close as twilight sings,
Dwindling light, the night's caress,
In its hold, we find our rest.

Remnant Radiance

In the stillness of the night,
Lingers remnant, softest light,
Fleeting beams of times long past,
In the shadows, shadows cast.

Hues of gold and amber soared,
Traces of what once adored,
In their glow, a remnant's plea,
Of what was, and what shall be.

Memories in beams ensnared,
Moments felt, but none repaired,
Ghostly light that dances slow,
In its glimmer, stories glow.

Echoes in this fading gleam,
Fragments of a distant dream,
In their softness, whispers weave,
Traces only night can grieve.

Thus we gather in the mist,
Folded in the shadows' kiss,
Remnant radiance, fading fast,
In its glow, the night is cast.

Burnt Echoes

Fires burned with fierce delight,
Turning dawn to darkest night,
From the flames, the echoes rise,
Woven through the midnight skies.

Voices lost in ashes spread,
Tales of those who went ahead,
In the embers, whispers stay,
Traces of another day.

Echoes through the starlit veil,
Silent secrets, quiet trails,
Messages from long ago,
In their flicker, glimpses show.

Life and loss in every spark,
Painting light upon the dark,
Burnt echoes in the midnight air,
Hope and sorrow mingled there.

In the silence, shadows speak,
Of the bold and of the meek,
Burnt echoes, a call to know,
What remains when embers glow.

Waning Fires

The embers shiver in twilight's grasp,
As day succumbs to night's tight clasp,
Fleeting warmth of a once bright past,
Fades into shadows, dark and vast.

Crimson glow, now smoldered low,
Whispers tales of ember's woe,
In the still of night their stories grow,
Of passions lost in ember's flow.

Dreams dissolving in the mist,
Of time's relentless, fading kiss,
A dance of sparkles, twirl and twist,
Into darkness, they desist.

Silent echoes in the breeze,
Rustling leaves among the trees,
Remnants of fire's fervent pleas,
Now adrift on memory's seas.

In the ashes, truths reside,
Of tempests passed, now pacified,
Waning fires by hopes still tied,
To embers' glow, though dreams have died.

Incandescent Echoes

Lights reflected in water's calm,
Whispers of an ancient psalm,
Softly burns a wordless charm,
Guarding nights from fears that swarm.

Flickers paint the velvet sky,
Scattered rays which softly sigh,
Echoed dreams that voice a cry,
For moments pure, that swiftly fly.

Glows that glide through midnight's veil,
Singing songs of long lost trails,
In the dark, where hopes prevail,
Incandescent echoes sail.

Specters of the morning dew,
Gleaming silently anew,
Carrying dreams both fierce and true,
To where the starlight cleaves the blue.

Echoes shimmer, faintly bright,
Guiding through the shadowed night,
Softly burning, gentle light,
Chasing shadows out of sight.

Warmth of Afterglow

Sunset paints the sky with gold,
Stories of the day retold,
In hues so warm, their truth unfolds,
Within the afterglow, a world to hold.

Memories linger in the light,
Reflections dancing in twilight,
Softly drawn by fading sight,
Embraced by colors, tender, bright.

In the dusk, soft voices weave,
Tales that hearts can scarce believe,
As the night's veil starts to cleave,
To dreams and hopes we won't conceive.

Warmth of moments, gently fade,
Carried by the night's parade,
Tinted with the twilight's shade,
In afterglow, our truths are made.

Whispers soft on evening's tide,
In the glow, our souls confide,
Holding close what hearts abide,
Beneath the afterglow, we hide.

Scorched Eternities

Amid the ruins, time stands still,
Echoes of a fiery will,
Where once bright flames did hearts fulfill,
Now memories the voids do fill.

Scorched earth tells of days gone by,
Burning bright beneath the sky,
Passionate as stars on high,
Now into ashes, dreams do lie.

Resilience in the charred remains,
Silent whispers through the plains,
Through the scorch, hope still refrains,
Amidst the echoes of past pains.

Eternity in flames' embrace,
Leaves a mark time can't erase,
Scarring deeply on each face,
A memory of fierce grace.

In the ashes, seeds of lore,
From scorched earth new dreams restore,
In the silence, hearts implore,
For growth to spring forevermore.

Hushed Hearth

In quiet corners dimly cast,
Where shadows meld with time's swift pass,
A hearth once full, now softly sleeps,
Its silence cloaks what secrets keep.

Through winters' chill and summers' grace,
The hearth once warmed each cherished face,
Now silence reigns, the embers cold,
Yet memories of warmth unfold.

From whispered tales and laughter's spark,
The hushed hearth holds a tender mark,
Each flicker gone, but whispers stay,
In hearts where love's soft echoes play.

Beneath the ash, a spark may gleam,
In dreams returned, in memories seen,
For even still, in quiet's breath,
The hushed hearth bears its marks of death.

Yet through the silent, empty room,
One feels the warmth that used to bloom,
In every shadow, every shade,
The hushed hearth's gentle glow displayed.

Shimmering Traces

Beneath the moon's soft glowing sweep,
Where silent waters lull and leap,
The shimmering traces softly draw,
A dance of light, a silent awe.

Across the sky, a trail of stars,
Whispers of light from realms afar,
They shimmer soft, then fade away,
But traces of their gleam will stay.

In each reflection, each refract,
The traces weave a shining pact,
To linger long, though time may wane,
Their sparkling truths in hearts remain.

A firefly's brief, tender glow,
A comet's sweep in evening's show,
Each holds a trace, a fleeting flash,
Of moments bright, then gently pass.

So here within this twilight's grace,
We find the shimmering traces' place,
In every glance, each silent sigh,
Their light remains, though they may fly.

Bygone Sparks

In corridors where echoes tread,
The bygone sparks from fires dead,
They dance in memories, bright and clear,
Though time has passed, they're ever near.

Each spark a tale, a laughter shared,
A whispered wish, a moment dared,
Though now they slumber, cold and still,
Their light ignites in memory's thrill.

Across the years, the sparks will fly,
Like constellations in the sky,
They guide us through the darkest night,
These lingering traces of pure light.

In silenced rooms where shadows fall,
The bygone sparks, they still recall,
The warmth of touch, the gaze of love,
Their radiant glow, once bright above.

So keep these sparks within your heart,
Though fires fade, they won't depart,
For in the darkened halls of mind,
The bygone sparks you still will find.

Vestiges of Flame

Where once the roaring fires blazed,
Now only vestiges are traced,
In charred remains of what had shone,
The remnants of a fire's tone.

Each ember holds a story told,
Of passions fierce and spirits bold,
Though flames have waned and light has flown,
Their essence lingers, partly known.

In quiet ashes, whispers speak,
Of moments brief, of futures bleak,
Yet in these vestiges, we find,
A spark of hope, a flame confined.

Through winter's bite and summer's heat,
The vestiges of flame will meet,
To tell their tales of times long gone,
When fires burned from dusk till dawn.

So heed the lessons flames impart,
In every ember lies the heart,
Of all that was and all that's been,
The vestiges of flame within.

Evocative Embers

In flames that softly fold and bow,
The stories of the past ignite,
Each ember tells a tale somehow,
Of memories in soft twilight.

The amber glow of days gone by,
Where laughter drifted, light as air,
A whisper in the smoky sky,
Of moments gone, yet still they're there.

Crackling songs in ember's dance,
Echoes of love and pain entwined,
In ash and flame, a second chance,
To glimpse what's left behind the mind.

In burning coals, so brightly splayed,
The shadows of old dreams appear,
Evocative, these embers laid,
To warm the heart and chase the fear.

For in each spark, a soul's embrace,
In gleam and glow, a time misplaced,
In smoldering dusk, find our grace,
Evocative embers interlaced.

Burnt Time

In the cinders of forgotten days,
Chronicles of time stand still,
Burnt edges of paper, threadbare stays,
Echoes of moments, past's goodwill.

Ashes drift where clocks won't chime,
Eroding whispers of the years,
Time is burnt, yet still sublime,
In silent tears and masked cheers.

Scorched relics of the heart's delight,
Charred by passion's fleeting fire,
In embers lost, yet vividly bright,
Recall the pyres of deep desire.

The canvas of the years we braid,
Each stroke a flame, each time remade,
Burnt memories in twilight fade,
In shadows cast by time's cascade.

Through the haze of burnt-out flame,
Seek the pulse within the char,
For in this dance of time we claim,
The light of who and where we are.

Old Fire's Tale

By the hearth where stories linger,
Old flames flicker in the night,
With a touch of memory's finger,
In the glow of warm twilight.

Whispers weave through ancient fire,
Tales of distant, storied past,
Embers glow with silent choir,
In their light, the shadows cast.

Each crackle tells a lover's plight,
Fables etched in flame's embrace,
Old fire's tale, in flickered light,
Reflections of a forgotten place.

Echoes live in burned-out wood,
Songs of sorrow and of joy,
Old fire's tale is understood,
By hearts unburdened with decoy.

As the flames fade, gentle, slow,
Their stories melding with the night,
In the heart, old fires glow,
A tale retold in every light.

Whispers of Yesteryears

In the sigh of winds that wander,
Through the halls of yesterday,
Lie whispers of the times fonder,
Sunlit scenes that fade away.

Echoes of a laughter's sweet,
In the corners of the mind,
Whispers of those past times meet,
In dreams where heart and time unwind.

Shadows long of stories spun,
By the hearth of memory's glow,
Yesteryears in whispers run,
Paths of which we still don't know.

In the silence of the night,
Hear the whispers soft and clear,
Of the days in golden light,
Fading, though forever dear.

Through the years, the whispers trace,
The echoes of a fleeting grace,
In their song, find tender space,
To hold the past in soft embrace.

Dust of Days

In the quiet of the evening blaze,
Memories twist and softly haze,
Ancient whispers fill the air,
Leaving marks we barely bear.

Footsteps echo on empty roads,
Stories etched in time's abode,
Sunsets blend in amber hue,
Moments lost but ever true.

Veils of dusk in twilight spread,
Dreams are woven, softly tread,
Dust of days in gentle flow,
Past and present warmly glow.

Glimmering thoughts from time's embrace,
Fading swiftly, leave no trace,
Shadows dance in night's serene,
Silent echoes, softly keen.

Down the corridors of space and time,
Whispers linger, sweet and fine,
Winds of change that softly play,
Stir the dust of bygone day.

Glow of Yore

Beneath the arch of twilight's firm,
Olden tales in hearts do squirm,
Echoes bright from days before,
Bathed in gentle glow of yore.

Lanterns glint in moonlit skies,
Drawing forth the heart's soft sighs,
Shadows long and stories old,
In their grasp, the warmth they hold.

Days of gold in memories cast,
Stretching forth from shadows vast,
Sparkling threads of time traverse,
Binding hearts in silent verse.

Ancient embers, softly lit,
Guide us through the night's cool wit,
Glow of yore, relentless gleam,
Bridges time by starlight's beam.

In the hush of night's ascent,
Fantasies and dreams are lent,
To the winds of time that soar,
Whispering the glow of yore.

Illuminated Past

Underneath the silent stars,
Time reveals its endless scars,
Illuminated past unfolds,
Stories of the brave and bold.

Olden skies with silver hue,
Guiding paths we once knew,
Candles lit in memories vast,
Lighting up the ages past.

Fallen leaves in autumn's grip,
Silent tales from time's vast crypt,
Beckon forth in glows so clear,
Echoes of a yesteryear.

Through the mists of time and rain,
Glimpses of the past's refrain,
Gently woven, softly cast,
Into the illuminated past.

Memories like a whisper's song,
Softly trailing, ever long,
In the glow of twilight vast,
Lies the illuminated past.

Silent Sparks

In the stillness of the night,
Silent sparks begin their flight,
Flickering dreams take to the sky,
Whispering wonders soft and shy.

Ancient fires, softly gleam,
Painting life in silver streams,
Patterns form in quiet arcs,
In the dance of silent sparks.

Ripples through the silent air,
Echoed thoughts and tendered care,
Wishes soar in gentle larks,
Guided by the silent sparks.

Moments etched in calm repose,
Hidden truths that softly glow,
In the night, the heart embarks,
On a journey through silent sparks.

Glistening in the starlit dark,
Dreams ignite with tender spark,
Following the night's cool marks,
Wander with the silent sparks.

Moments in Smoke

In twilight's embrace, the silence grows,
Whispers in the air, where the ember shows.
A fleeting moment, a wisp of thought,
In the smoky veil, a dream is caught.

Memories drift through the haze,
Lost in the labyrinth, a mystic maze.
Ephemeral joys of a timeless dance,
Captured in the ashes, a stolen glance.

Softly fades the evening light,
Echoes of laughter in the dimly-lit night.
Shadows trace a gentle curve,
Stories told in the smoke that swerve.

A phantom touch, a lingering kiss,
In the corners of our hearts' abyss.
Time dissolves in the smoky tide,
Where love and dreams quietly reside.

The night stretches on, serene and cool,
As smoke twines around the moonlit pool.
In the end, with sighs unspoke,
We find our truth in moments of smoke.

Yesterday's Flames

In the glow of forgotten fires,
Lie the echoes of old desires.
Embers of a yesterday, now tame,
Whisper secrets through the flame.

Flickers dance on shadows' edge,
Stories etched on life's thin ledge.
Once fierce light now softly wanes,
Memories sing in yesterday's flames.

Each spark a tale of days gone by,
Woven in the star-clad sky.
Time's caress now gently frames,
The tender warmth of yesterday's flames.

In the quiet, hearts rekindle,
To the thoughts that never dwindle.
Past and present, all the same,
In the gentle kiss of yesterday's flame.

We gather close and softly sigh,
Underneath a wistful sky.
In reverie, our souls reclaim,
The golden touch of yesterday's flame.

Shadows and Sparks

Night's blanket thick and dark,
Pierced by dreams, like a spark.
In the interplay of light and shade,
Shadows and sparks are artful, made.

A silent whisper through the woods,
Stirring ancient, sleeping moods.
In silhouette, our fears embark,
Caught between the shadows and sparks.

The firelight dances, wild and free,
Reflecting all that we wish to be.
A spark of hope, the dark disarms,
In shadows, we find tender charms.

Each glint a bold, igniting flare,
In the dusky, cooling air.
As darkness gently leaves its mark,
We wander through shadows and sparks.

In this ballet of night and light,
We find our strength, our quiet might.
Together we make our poignant marks,
Eternal souls in shadows and sparks.

Flickers of the Heart

Beneath a moonlit, starry sky,
Our secret wishes softly fly.
In the tender glow, where dreams depart,
Lie the gentle flickers of the heart.

Each beat a pulse of endless song,
In its cadence, we belong.
Promises made, never to part,
In the warm flickers of the heart.

The world may turn, with time's cruel hand,
But love's light forever will stand.
In every kiss, a brand new start,
Guided by the flicker in the heart.

In the shadows, doubts may creep,
Yet through the night, our love will sweep.
Trust and faith will play their part,
Strengthened by the flickers of the heart.

Together we will light our way,
Through every night and every day.
With love's unending, radiant spark,
In the eternal flickers of the heart.

Persuasive Pyres

In twilight's gentle, soothing light,
Where ashes dance and embers bright,
The pyres whisper, tales anew,
Of hopes and dreams, in flickered hue.

From ancient woods, they rise and sing,
A chorus bound by fire's ring,
Their warmth, a balm, to night's embrace,
These pyres persuade with tender grace.

The dancing flames, like ribbon streams,
Entwine with shadows, weaving dreams,
Persuasive pyres, with voices low,
Recite our past, their wisdom's glow.

Amid the stars, the sparks ascend,
A fleeting touch of realms, transcend,
In pyres' song, we find our place,
A fleeting glimpse of time and space.

So gather close, 'round glowing hearth,
For pyres' tales of joy and mirth,
Persuasive whispers, gentle sway,
Guide us through the night to day.

Historic Flickers

Upon the stage of bygone years,
Historic flickers, bright and clear,
Their shadows stretch through time and space,
Illuminating every face.

In echoes far, their stories told,
Of legends grand and heroes bold,
Through flickers' light, the past returns,
Where hearts once burned, our spirit learns.

Beneath the shroud of twilight's gleam,
History's whispers softly stream,
Flickers dance on walls and stones,
Recounting lives, their joys and moans.

The ancient flames, a guiding star,
Through corridors of time so far,
Flickers paint the nights of old,
Unveil secrets, tales untold.

Amidst the glow, we intertwine,
With centuries, a sacred line,
Historic flickers, bring to light,
The endless dance of time's twilight.

Luminary Ashes

From fiery birth to ashen end,
Luminary lights descend,
Their shadows stretch, a stellar trace,
Through night they whisper, silent grace.

Amidst the dark, their embers rise,
To kiss the stars, the cosmic ties,
Ashes fly, on wings of night,
Guiding dreams with gentle sight.

In ash and spark, the stories dwell,
Of ancient lore and distant spell,
Luminaries of both earth and sky,
Their legacy we can't deny.

The ashes hold a soft embrace,
Of dreams and hopes we can't replace,
Through luminary shades they cast,
Reflecting futures and the past.

So gather 'round, and heed the call,
Of luminary nights that fall,
In ashes, find the sparks that cling,
To every end, a new beginning.

Evocative Blaze

In the heart of night, the blaze ascends,
Evoking tales through bends and trends,
A brilliant light that cuts so deep,
It rouses dreams from silent sleep.

Through forests dense and cities grand,
The blaze reaches with a guiding hand,
Its flames call forth the spirits bound,
In evocations, truths are found.

On fields of war and lands of peace,
The blaze speaks of endless release,
Evocative, it shapes our fate,
With every spark, a whispered state.

The colors bright in pyro's dance,
Remind us of life's fleeting chance,
Evoking hearts to seek and find,
The flames within, a kindred bind.

So as you watch the blaze take flight,
Let it evoke a deeper sight,
For in each flume and fiery gaze,
Lies the soul of life's embrace.